DO YOU WANT TO KEEP YOUR CUSTOMERS FOREVER?

Harvard Business Review
CLASSICS

DO YOU WANT TO KEEP YOUR CUSTOMERS FOREVER?

B. Joseph Pine II, Don Peppers, and
Martha Rogers

Harvard Business Press
Boston, Massachusetts

THE HARVARD BUSINESS
REVIEW CLASSICS SERIES

Since 1922, *Harvard Business Review* has
been a leading source of breakthrough ideas
in management practice—many of which still
speak to and influence us today. The HBR
Classics series now offers you the opportunity
to make these seminal pieces a part of your
permanent management library. Each volume
contains a groundbreaking idea that has
shaped best practices and inspired countless
managers around the world—and will change
how you think about the business world today.

DO YOU WANT TO KEEP YOUR CUSTOMERS FOREVER?

Customers, whether consumers or businesses, do not want more choices. They want exactly what they want—when, where, and how they want it—and technology now makes it possible for companies to give it to them. Interactive and database technology permits companies to amass huge amounts of data on individual customers' needs and preferences. And information technology and flexible manufacturing systems enable companies to customize large volumes of goods or services for individual customers at a relatively low cost. But few companies are exploiting this potential. Most managers continue to view the world through the twin lenses of mass marketing and mass production. To handle their increasingly turbulent and fragmented markets, they try to churn out a greater variety of goods and services and to target ever finer market segments with more tailored advertising messages. But these managers only end up bombarding their customers with too many choices.

A company that aspires to give customers exactly what they want must look at the world through new lenses. It must use technology to become two things: a *mass customizer* that efficiently provides individually customized goods and services, and a *one-to-one marketer* that elicits information from each customer about his or her specific needs and preferences. The twin logic of mass customization and one-to-one marketing binds producer and consumer together in what we call a *learning relationship*—an ongoing connection that becomes smarter as the two interact with each other, collaborating to meet the consumer's needs over time.

In learning relationships, individual customers teach the company more and more about their preferences and needs, giving the company an immense competitive advantage. The more customers teach the company, the better it becomes at providing exactly what they want—exactly how they want it—and the more difficult it will be for a competitor to entice them away. Even if a competitor were to build the exact same capabilities, a customer already involved in a learning relationship with the company would have to spend an inordinate amount of time and energy teaching the competitor what the company already knows.

Because of this singularly powerful competitive advantage, a company that can cultivate learning relationships with its customers should be able to retain their business virtually forever—provided that it continues to supply high-quality customized products or services at reasonably competitive prices and does not miss the next technology wave. (Learning relationships would not have saved a buggy-whip manufacturer from the automobile.)

One company that excels at building learning relationships with its customers is named, appropriately enough, Individual, Inc. This Burlington, Massachusetts, company, which competes with wire, clipping, and information-retrieval services, provides published news stories selected to fit the specific, ever changing interests of each client. Instead of having to sort through a mountain of clippings or having to master the arcane commands needed to search databases, Individual's customers—which include such diverse companies as MCI Telecommunications, McKinsey &

Company, Avon Products, and Fidelity Investments—effortlessly receive timely, fresh, relevant articles delivered right to their desks by fax, groupware (such as Lotus Notes), online computer services, the Internet, or electronic mail.

When someone signs up for Individual's *First!* service, the company assigns an editorial manager to determine what sort of information the client wants. The editorial manager and the client reduce those requests to simple descriptions, such as articles about new uses of information technology in home health care or about new products developed by Japanese semiconductor companies. The editorial manager enters the requests into Individual's

SMART software system (for System for Manipulation and Retrieval of Text). Then SMART takes over. Every business day, the system searches 400 sources containing more than 12,000 articles for those pieces that will most likely fit the client's needs, and it delivers them by whatever method the client has chosen.

Every week, Individual asks a new client (by fax or computer) to rate each article as "not relevant," "somewhat relevant," or "very relevant." The responses are fed into the system, making SMART even smarter. In the first week of service, most customers find only 40% to 60% of the articles to be somewhat or very relevant. By the fourth or fifth week, SMART has increased those ratings to a targeted 80% to 90%. Once it has achieved that level, Individual reduces the frequency of the ratings to once a month, which still enables it to keep abreast of customers' changing needs.

Individual also responds constantly to clients' requests for new sources and ways of receiving information. Sun Microsystems, for example, asked the company to place *First!* on its internal Internet server. Once Individual provided this service, it discovered that many other clients that also depended on the Internet for sending and sharing information wanted to receive the service in the same way. Such responsiveness is undoubtedly one reason why Individual, which has more than 30,000 users and more than 4,000 accounts, enjoys a customer-retention rate of 85% to 90%. But there is also another reason: because of the time and energy each client expends in teaching the company which articles are relevant and which are not, switching to a competitor would require the client to make that investment all over again.

FROM MASS PRODUCTION
TO MASS CUSTOMIZATION

Although Individual uses information and interactive technology to its fullest, most managers fail to understand that variety is not the same thing as customization. Customization means manufacturing a product or delivering a service *in response* to a particular customer's needs, and mass customization means doing it in a cost-effective way. Mass customization calls for a customer-centered orientation in production and delivery processes, requiring the company to collaborate with individual customers to design each one's desired product or service, which is then constructed from a base of pre-engineered modules that can be assembled in myriad ways.

In contrast, product-centered mass production and mass marketing call for pushing options (and inventory) into distribution channels and hoping that each new option is embraced by enough customers to make its production worthwhile. It requires customers to hunt for the single product or service they want from among an ever growing array of alternatives.

Consider grocery stores. According to *New Products News*, the number of new products, including line extensions, introduced in grocery stores each year increased from less than 3,000 in 1980 to more than 10,000 in 1988 and more than 17,000 in 1993. And *Progressive Grocer* reports that the number of stock-keeping units in the average supermarket doubled to more than 30,000 between 1980 and 1994. The same trend can be seen in many service industries: witness the proliferation of affinity credit cards and the numerous options offered by telephone companies.

Companies are also deluging consumers with a wider variety of messages. And, of course, there is a greater array of media for carrying them: direct mail, telemarketing, special newspaper supplements, and a larger number of television channels, among others.

For example, the average newspaper weighs 55% more today than it did just ten years ago, mainly because of supplements designed to carry specially targeted advertising. The problem with such supplements is that they are distributed to every subscriber. Nongardeners still receive the gardening supplement, and people reading the paper before heading to the office still get the work-at-home supplement. So the supplements really aren't so special after all.

Mass marketers use information technology to define the most likely customers for the products they want to sell. For the most part, the information comes from simple transactional records (such as customer purchases and invoices) and public information (such as vehicle registrations, address-change forms, and census data) compiled by companies like R.L. Polk and Donnelley Marketing. From those data, the mass marketer generates a list of the most likely prospects and solicits them with offers or messages that the marketer has attempted to customize by guessing their tastes. By contrast, the one-to-one marketer conducts a dialogue with each customer—one at a time—and uses the increasingly more detailed feedback to find the best products or services for that customer. Although many companies are moving toward this model, few have fully implemented it yet or combined it with mass customization.

Take Hallmark Cards and American Greetings, the leaders of the variety-intensive greeting card industry. Both companies have installed electronic kiosks in stores and other public places to enable people to create their own greeting cards. Consumers can touch the screen of either company's kiosk, quickly select the type of card they need (for example, anniversary or birthday card), browse through a number of selections, and then modify them or compose their own wording to express exactly the right sentiment. The card is printed in a minute or so.

Both companies seem pleased with the performance of their mass customization businesses, but neither has fully exploited its potential. The graphics for the cards are all preset (so only the wording can be customized), and there is little organization (so browsing through the choices can be time consuming). The greatest weakness of the electronic kiosks, however, is the absence of a system for recording individual customers' preferences. Each time someone uses the system, he or she must start all over again.

If a greeting card company were to harness the full power of mass customization and one-to-one marketing, it would be able to remember the important occasions in your life and remind you to buy a card. It would make suggestions based on your past purchases. Its kiosk would display past selections, either to ensure that you don't commit the faux pas of sending the same card to the same person twice or to give you the option of sending the same funny card to another person—appropriately personalized, of course. Perhaps the company would mail your cards or ship them across the Internet for you so they would arrive at the appointed time. Maybe the company would be able to remind you to send a card, allow you to design it, and arrange for its delivery on your personal computer through an on-line service that would let you incorporate your own graphics or photographs. It might even find your design so good that it would ask your permission to add it to its inventory.

Certainly, not every customer would want to invest the time that such a relationship would require. Neither would every customer buy enough cards to make such a relationship worthwhile for the company. But the advantages to a greeting card company of establishing and cultivating a learning relationship with customers who buy cards frequently are immense. Because every card sold to those customers will be tailored precisely to their needs, the company will be able to charge them a premium and its profit margins will increase. And because the company will be equipped to ensure that the customer never forgets an occasion, it will sell more cards to that customer. The company's product development will become more effective because of the expanded ability to understand exactly who is buying what, when, and why—not to mention the ability to use new ideas that customers could provide.

But, most important of all, the company will retain more customers, especially the most valuable ones: frequent purchasers. The more customers teach the company about their individual tastes, celebration occasions, and card recipients (addresses, relationships, and so forth), the more reluctant they will be to repeat that process with another supplier. As long as the company fulfills its end of the bargain, a competitor should never be able to entice away its customers. The battle will be limited to attracting new ones.

WHEN ARE LEARNING RELATIONSHIPS APPROPRIATE?

As compelling and powerful as the benefits of learning relationships are, this radically different business model cannot be applied in the same way by everyone. Companies such as home builders, real estate brokers, and appliance manufacturers—which do not interact frequently with end users—cannot learn enough to make a learning relationship with those customers work. But they might find it beneficial to develop such relationships with general contractors. Similarly, makers of products like paper clips, whose revenue or profit margin per customer is too low to justify building individual learning relationships with customers, might find it advantageous to cultivate learning relationships with office-supply chains, which interact directly with end users.

Even producers of commodities such as wheat or natural gas, which cannot be customized easily, and of commodity-like products bought mainly on the basis of price have much to gain from this approach. Learning relationships can enable such companies to design services that differentiate their offerings. This is the strategy that Bandag, which sells truck-tire retreads to more than 500 dealer-installers around the country, is pursuing.

Bandag's retreads are essentially a commodity because they are comparable in price and quality to those of competitors. To break out of the pack, Bandag is providing additional services. For example, it assists its dealers in filing and collecting on warranty claims from tire manufacturers and will soon begin offering comprehensive fleet-management services to its largest national accounts.

Bandag plans to embed computer chips in the rubber of newly retreaded tires to gauge each tire's pressure and temperature and to count its revolutions. That information will enable the company not only to tell each customer the optimal time to retread each tire (thus reducing downtime caused by blowouts) but also to help it improve its fleet's operations.

Because of the current high cost of building such capabilities, many manufacturers, service providers, and retailers may find, as Bandag did, that it pays to establish learning relationships only with their best customers. But as advances in information technology continue to drive down the cost of building learning relationships, they will make economic sense in many more businesses and for a wider spectrum of customers. Many types of industries are already ripe for revolution. They include the following.

Complex Products or Services

Most people do not want to work their way through hundreds or thousands of options, features, pricing structures, delivery methods, and networks to figure out which product or service is best for them. One solution is for companies to collaborate with customers in custom-designing the product, as Andersen Corporation, the window manufacturer based in Bayport, Minnesota, is doing. It resolved the information-overload problem for its customers (individual home owners and building contractors) by developing a multimedia system called the Window of Knowledge. A sales representative uses a workstation that features 50,000 possible window components to help customers design their own windows. The system automatically generates error-free quotations and manufacturing specifications, which can be saved for future use.

The resulting database of window configurations deepens Andersen's understanding of how its business is performing.

Big-Ticket Items

A company that succeeds in customizing all aspects of owning an expensive product or using a premium service stands to gain a competitive advantage over its rivals. Consider automobiles. A car buyer, over his or her lifetime, can generate hundreds of thousands of dollars' worth of business when financing, service, and referrals, as well as the original purchase, are taken into account. All together, they represent an enormous opportunity for companies that cater to customers' individual preferences.

The same opportunities apply to big-ticket commercial offerings, including machinery, information systems, outsourcing, and consulting. (See the box "How to Gain Customers Forever" at the end of the article.)

Digitizable Products and Services

Anything that can be digitized can be customized. If such products are purchased frequently, providing a discernible pattern of personal preferences, they may be ideally suited for one-to-one marketing as well. Obvious candidates include not only greeting cards but also software, periodicals, telecommunication services, and entertainment products such as movies, videos, games, and recorded music. Indeed, many companies in these businesses are working to develop learning relationships.

On-Line Services

Providers of on-line services already offer a broad spectrum of choices—including electronic shopping, special-interest forums, entertainment, news, and financial services—but few offer tailored convenience. Currently, the user must navigate through choice after choice. A competitor that learns a customer's wants and needs could navigate cyberspace on behalf of that customer and cull only the relevant choices.

Luxury and Specialty Products

Many businesses (such as apparel, perfume and cosmetics, athletic equipment, and fine wine) have customers with complex individual tastes. For example, people differ not only in their physical measurements but also in how they prefer their clothes to fit and look. Levi Strauss is capitalizing on these differences by mass-customizing blue jeans for women, using technology supplied by Custom Clothing Technology Corporation of Newton, Massachusetts. After a customer has her measurements taken in a store, she tries on a pair or two of jeans to determine her exact preference. The information is then sent to the factory for prompt production. Although Levi Strauss is currently limiting the program to one style of jeans, the approach offers the company tremendous opportunities for building learning relationships.

Retailing Services

In many industries, retailers have a big advantage over manufacturers in building learning relationships with end users, especially when customers want to touch, feel, and browse (clothing, shoes, and books) or when the product is immediately consumed (for example, in restaurants and bars). They also have the edge when individual customers do not buy a large amount of any one manufacturer's products (such as groceries and packaged goods). That is because the retailer is in a better position to see patterns in a customer's purchases and because it might be more expensive for the manufacturer to build learning relationships. Finally, many retailers offer consumers not products per se but service, and services can be mass-customized more readily than most products can. (See the box "How Peapod Is Customizing the Virtual Supermarket" at the end of the article)

VYING FOR THE END CUSTOMER

Retailers, insurance agents, distributors, interior decorators, building contractors, and others who deal face-to-face with the end customer can certainly make the case that they should be the ones who control the relationship with that customer. On the other hand, manufacturers and service providers have an advantage when a customer often buys the same type of product (toiletries, magazines, or office supplies); when products can be economically delivered to the home or office (personal computers, software, or services such as lawn care and plumbing); or when customers already value their relationship with the product or brand (as with premium Scotch, designer jeans, or luxury watches).

Obviously, those boundaries are permeable and constantly shifting: manufacturers and service providers can become retailers and vice versa. And advances in technology are making it increasingly easy for one member of the value chain to undermine another's natural advantages. Consider, for example, three basic reasons consumers go to retail stores: to obtain the information they need to make a purchasing decision, to pay for the product, and to take possession of it. Thanks to the same information-based technologies that make learning relationships possible, consumers increasingly will not have to visit stores for any of those reasons.

Today, consumers can get better information—information that is unbiased, comparative, accurate, and immediate— through on-line services, CD-ROM catalogs, and fax-response systems, and eventually they will be able to obtain it through interactive TV. As the continuing boom in catalog and home-TV shopping attests, consumers and organizations can buy goods and services over the phone and through dedicated on-line services as easily as, if not more easily than, in person, and security measures will almost certainly be in place soon that will make it possible to purchase products through the Internet. Finally, almost anything can be delivered direct to the home thanks to Federal Express, UPS, dedicated delivery services, and (for digitized products) fax and on-line services.

For retailers, the message is clear: if they want to maintain or increase their competitive advantage, they must begin establishing learning relationships with their best customers today. On the other hand, a manufacturer or a service company one or more links removed from the end user has a variety of options. It could build collaborative learning relationships with those occupying the next link, gaining knowledge about their wants, needs, and preferences over time, and mass-customizing products and services to meet their requirements. That is the approach ITT Hartford's Personal Lines business is taking with the independent agents who sell its automobile and home insurance. And it is also the direction in which Andersen—which realizes that individual home owners buy windows too infrequently to form a productive, long-term relationship with the company—is heading. Although Andersen plans to continue to mass-customize windows for consumers, it also intends to cultivate learning relationships with architects, home builders, and window distributors.

Another option for a manufacturer or a service company is to form tighter partnerships with retailers so that together they control the learning relationships with individual end customers. Such a partnership would require sharing information and knowledge (and maybe a common database), linking operations tightly so consumers' desires could be translated efficiently and quickly into tailored products and services, and possibly making joint investment and strategic decisions on how best to serve end customers over time. This option might make sense for companies such as automakers, which rely heavily on dealers to provide the touch, feel, and test drive necessary for consumers to make a buying decision.

HOW TO BUILD LEARNING RELATIONSHIPS

If managers decide that their company can and should cultivate learning relationships with customers, how do they go about it? There are basically four components to think about: an *information strategy* for initiating dialogues with customers and remembering their preferences; a *production/delivery strategy* for fulfilling what the company learns about individual customers; an *organizational strategy* for managing both customers and capabilities; and an *assessment strategy* for evaluating performance.

The Information Strategy

Cultivating learning relationships depends on a company's ability to elicit and manage information about customers. The first step is to identify those individual customers with whom it pays to have a learning relationship. That is easy for businesses like hotels or airlines, whose customers make reservations in their own names and whose transactions and preferences are easy to track.

In industries whose customers are anonymous, such as retailing, a company may have to use one of two approaches to persuade them to identify and provide information about themselves: show them that it can serve them better if they do or give them something of value in return, such as a gift or a discount. For example, Waldenbooks offers a 10% discount on all purchases if customers identify themselves by becoming Preferred Readers. The program allows the company to track the purchases of those customers at any Waldenbooks store. Learning about customer preferences enables the bookseller to let a particular customer know when, for example, the next William Styron novel will be out or when an author whose work the customer has purchased will be in a local store, signing books.

Few companies will want to have such relationships with all customers. Waldenbooks' program, for example, is aimed at people who spend more than $100 a year at its stores. As a screening device, the company charges a $10 annual fee for Preferred Reader status.

As with any new program, it is often best to begin with a company's most valuable customers. When the company sees that the value of a learning relationship with them exceeds the costs, it can gradually expand the program to other customers.

Once a company has identified the customers with whom it wishes to have a learning relationship, there are a number of ways in which it can conduct a productive dialogue. A rapidly expanding array of interactive technologies—including electronic kiosks, on-line services, and database-driven mail—are making such dialogues easier and less costly. (See the box "How to Interact: A Sampler of Today's Technologies" at the end of the article.) Businesses that naturally involve personal contact with customers, either on the phone or in person, have golden opportunities to learn about them.

In conducting a dialogue with customers, it is important that the database "remember" not just preferences declared in past purchases but also the preferences that emerge from questions, complaints, suggestions, and actions.

The Ritz-Carlton hotel chain trains all its associates—from those on the front desk to those in maintenance and housekeeping—how to converse with customers and how to handle complaints immediately. In addition, it provides each associate with a "guest preference pad" for writing down every preference gleaned from conversations with and observations of customers. Every day, the company enters those preferences into a chainwide database that now contains profiles of nearly a half million patrons. Employees at any of the 28 Ritz-Carlton hotels worldwide can gain access to those profiles through the Covia travel-reservation system.

Say you stay at the Ritz-Carlton in Cancún, Mexico, call room service for dinner, and request an ice cube in your glass of white wine. Months later, when you stay at the Ritz-Carlton in Naples, Florida, and order a glass of white wine from room service, you will almost certainly be asked if you would like an ice cube in it. The same would be true if you asked for a window seat in a restaurant, a minibar with no liquor in your room, or a variety of other necessities or preferences that personalize your stay at the Ritz-Carlton.

By retaining such information, a company becomes better equipped to respond to suggestions, resolve complaints, and stay abreast of customers' changing needs. Many companies make the mistake of treating customers as if they were static entities rather than people whose preferences, lifestyles, and circumstances are constantly evolving and shifting.

Some managers may wonder whether customers will see requests for in-depth personal information as an invasion of privacy.

Most people don't mind divulging their shopping habits, measurements, and friends' names and addresses if they believe they're getting something of value in return. Consumers' fears also will be assuaged if a company states unequivocally that it will jealously guard personal information, which any company building learning relationships must do. Unlike mass marketers, who buy and sell customer data willy-nilly, companies seeking to build learning relationships realize that such information is a precious asset.

The Production/Delivery Strategy

Children can create an unlimited number of unique designs with Lego building blocks.

Service and manufacturing companies that have successfully mass-customized employ a similar approach: they create modules—components or processes—that can be assembled in a variety of ways to enable the companies to tailor products or services for specific customers at a relatively low cost. (See B. Joseph Pine II, Bart Victor, and Andrew C. Boynton, "Making Mass Customization Work," HBR September–October 1993.) Admittedly, there is more opportunity to adopt this approach in some businesses than in others. For example, the Ritz-Carlton is more of a customizer than a mass customizer. If it could figure out how to mass-customize its services, as Peapod has done, it would be able to cater to the preferences of more of its customers *and* increase its profits.

However, creating process or component modules is not enough. A company also needs a design tool that can take a customer's requirements and easily determine how to use its capabilities to fulfill them. Individual, Inc.'s SMART system and Andersen's Window of Knowledge system are examples of design tools that enable companies to be as effective as possible in ascertaining what customers need, as efficient as possible in production and delivery, and as effortless as possible in matching the two.

The Organizational Strategy

Traditional marketing organizations depend on product managers to push the product out the door, into the channels, and into customers' hands. Product managers are generally responsible for performing market research, specifying the requirements for a fairly standardized offering, and developing the marketing plan. And once the product is introduced, they are rewarded for selling as much of it as possible. While these techniques are ideally suited for mass marketing, they are ill suited for learning relationships in which the reverse is required: extracting a customer's wants and needs from a dialogue and creating the product or service that fulfills those requirements.

To build learning relationships, companies don't need product managers; they need *customer managers*. As the term implies, customer managers oversee the relationship with the customer. While they are responsible for a portfolio of customers with similar needs, they also are responsible for obtaining all the business possible from *each* customer, one at a time. To do this, customer managers must know their customers' preferences and be able to help them articulate their needs. They serve as gatekeepers within the company for all communication to and from each customer.

In addition, companies need *capability managers*, each of whom executes a distinct production or delivery process for fulfilling each customer's requirements. The head of each capability ensures that appropriate capacity exists and that the process can be executed reliably and efficiently.

Customer managers must know what capability managers can provide and must take the lead in determining when new capabilities may be required to meet customers' needs. For their part, capability managers must know what customer managers require and be able to figure out how to create it. For instance, when a Peapod customer informed his customer manager (a Membership Services representative) that he wanted to be able to order both ripe and unripe tomatoes, the company expanded the capabilities of its ordering software and created a new set of capability managers: produce specialists. These specialists have the skills and experience to squeeze tomatoes and thump melons, for example. Similarly, a customer manager at four year-old Individual asked the company's manager of information suppliers—the capability manager responsible for managing and acquiring new sources of information—to add the *New England Journal of Medicine* after learning that a client needed articles from the publication. Individual expands the number of its sources by 75 to 100 per year in this manner.

In contrast to the traditional product manager's role of finding customers for the company's products, the role of the customer manager is finding products for the company's customers. Often, a customer manager will learn of a need for some product or service component that the organization does not consider itself competent to produce or deliver. The capability manager might then arrange to obtain it from a strategic partner or a third-party vendor. For example, it would not pay for AT & T's computer hardware and software business, AT & T Global Information Solutions (formerly NCR), to write software for every conceivable customer need. When a customer-focused team (the unit's equivalent of customer managers) learns that a customer needs a particular application that is unavailable in-house, it often asks a capability-management team to acquire or license the software.

In all cases, however, the customer manager must be held accountable for satisfying the customer. At ITT Hartford's Personal

Lines business, every time a customer (an independent agent) makes a request, Personal Lines forms an instant team composed of people from whichever service modules (underwriting, claims payment, or servicing, for example) are needed to satisfy the request. But the customer manager is the one responsible for guaranteeing the promised customized service. He or she specifies the commitment to the agent at the beginning of each transaction, and a tracking system ensures that it is fulfilled.

The Assessment Strategy

Obviously, the value of a learning relationship to the company will vary from customer to customer. Some customers will be more willing than others to invest the time and effort. Those willing to participate are going to have a wide variety of demands or expectations, meaning that the company will have a varying ability to contribute to and profit from each relationship. Companies should therefore decide which potential learning relationships they will pursue.

The ideal way to approach this task is to think about a customer's lifetime value. Lifetime value is the sum of the future stream of profits and other benefits attributable to all purchases and transactions with an individual customer, discounted back to its present value. In their article "Zero Defections: Quality Comes to Services" (HBR September–October 1990), Frederick F. Reichheld and W. Earl Sasser, Jr., showed that the longer customers are retained by a company, the more profitable they become because of increased purchases, reduced operating costs, referrals, price premiums, and reduced customer acquisition costs. We would add one more element to the list: some customers will have higher lifetime values because the insights they provide to the company may result in new capabilities that can be applied to other customers. Although it is a daunting task, companies seeking to build learning relationships should therefore try to track as many of those elements as they can, using such information as transactional histories and customer feedback.

A company's *customer share*—its share of each customer's total patronage—is one of the most useful measures of success in building a learning relationship. To calculate customer share, a company must have some idea of what the customer is buying from the competition and what he or she might be willing to buy from the company. The best source of such information is the customer—another reason why dialogue is critical.

Yet another important performance measure is what we call *customer sacrifice*: the gap between what each customer truly wants and needs and what the company can supply. To understand individual customer sacrifice, companies building learning relationships must go beyond the aggregate customer-satisfaction figures that almost everyone collects today. That is why Peapod asks every customer at every shopping session how well it did on the last order. Understanding and tracking this gap will enable customer managers to demonstrate the need for new capabilities to deepen learning relationships and will give capability managers the information they need to decide how to expand or change their company's capabilities.

BECOMING A LEARNING BROKER

After a company becomes adept at cultivating learning relationships with its current customers, how might it expand?

Two choices are obvious: acquire new customers in the company's current markets or expand into new locations. But there is a third option: deliver *other* products to *current* customers and become a learning broker.

Because Peapod's customers already know how to interact with its on-line ordering system, the company could easily broker new product categories. For example, if Peapod could gain entry into a chain of home-improvement centers (meaning on-line access to the chain's computerized list of stock-keeping units and prices, and Peapod shoppers' access to the stores themselves), its knowledge about its customers and its customers' knowledge about it would immediately transfer to a whole new set of "virtual aisles." And once again, it would be Peapod—not the chains or the manufacturers that supply them—that would control the relationship with the customers. By arbitraging the information between customers and companies that supply products and services that they could potentially use, Peapod would have become a bona fide learning broker.

Discussions of what life will be like in the information-rich, interactive future often focus on personal electronic "agents" that will watch out for each individual's information and entertainment needs, sifting and sorting through the plethora of channels, messages, and offerings. But the dynamics of

learning relationships are such that learning
brokers can provide that service today in
a wide variety of domains. They could provide individual customers with products and
services beyond those that their companies
have traditionally supplied. They also could
advise their customers about other offerings
and be on the lookout for items they
might want.

One of the best examples of a company
that already serves its customers in this
fashion is the United Services Automobile
Association. Seventy years ago, USAA began
providing automobile insurance to military
officers. It now supplies its customers—
whom it still limits to current and former
military officers and their families—with a

wide variety of products and services. They include all types of insurance, full-service banking, investment brokerage, homes in retirement communities, and travel services. USAA also offers a buying service through which it purchases and delivers other companies' products, including automobiles, jewelry, major appliances, and consumer electronics. The relationship with the customer, however, remains the sole dominion of USAA.

USAA members have learned over the years that the company stands behind everything it sells and looks after their best interests. As more than one member has said, USAA could sell almost anything to them. More than nine of every ten active-duty and former military officers are members. And since opening up its services to members' adult children in the 1970s, USAA has been able to attract more than half of them, showing that learning relationships can even span generations.

The role of a learning broker clearly makes sense for distributors or agents such as Peapod and Individual, two companies that make no products themselves. Such companies are relatively free to go to whatever company can provide exactly what their customers want and need. Whether to take the path of a learning broker is a more complex decision for a manufacturer or a service company. But it is not out of the question. A company can become a hybrid like

USAA: it offers its members a wide variety of other companies' products, but, in its core business, financial services, it offers only its own products. While it may be difficult to imagine today, many companies could eventually decide that it pays to become a learning broker even of competitors' products. But adopting that strategy will make sense only if a company reaches the point where its knowledge of its customers and their trust in it yield a greater competitive advantage and greater profits than merely selling its own products can. When that happens, learning relationships with end customers will have become the company's primary competency.

How to Gain Customers Forever

Industrial companies that sell to other businesses can benefit just as much from learning relationships as companies that sell products or services to consumers. Consider the case of Ross Controls (formerly the Ross Operating Valve Company) of Troy, Michigan, a 70-year-old manufacturer of pneumatic valves and air-control systems. Through what it calls the ROSS/FLEX process, Ross learns about its customers' needs, collaborates with them to come up with designs precisely tailored to help them meet those needs, and quickly and efficiently makes the customized products. The process has enabled the medium-size manufacturer to forge learning relationships with such companies as General Motors, Knight Industries, Reynolds Aluminum, and Japan's Yamamura Glass.

For example, Ross is currently supplying GM's Metal Fabricating Division with 600 integrated-valve systems. Based on a common platform but individually customized for a particular stamping press, each integrated system performs better than the valves it is replacing at one-third the price.

Two elements have enabled Ross to transform itself from a sleepy industrial manufacturer into a dynamic organization that cultivates learning relationships with its customers.

A Desire to Listen to and Collaborate with Each Customer

This involves spending time on the phone, faxing ideas back and forth, and often visiting plants to see how pneumatic systems are to be used in the customer's manufacturing process. And once a system is designed to solve the customer's problem, Ross gets feedback from prototypes and encourages the customer to make continuous upgrades to its valve designs, yielding more precisely tailored designs over time. Ross then stores them in a library of design platforms, components, and computer instructions for its manufacturing equipment so it does not have to start from scratch every time it works with a customer on a new project.

The Capability to Turn Complex Designs into Products

Through the effective use of computer-aided design (CAD) and computer numerically controlled (CNC) machines, Ross can electronically transmit tooling instructions directly from engineering workstations to multimillion-dollar production equipment, which can turn around new designs in as little as a day. But obviously, computer-aided-design and manufacturing equipment alone does not enable a company to mass-customize. Information about each customer's needs is also essential. To obtain such information, Ross created a crew of "integrators," each of whom is assigned to a given customer. The integrator talks with the customer, produces the valve designs, and determines the manufacturing specifications, including the instructions for the CNC machines. Using the CAD system, the integrator draws from the library's contents whenever possible to create a customized design and the computer coding required to make the product.

The ROSS/FLEX process has helped Ross boost the custom portion of its business from 5% to 20% of its revenues in the past four years. But the company is not yet satisfied with its ability to build learning relationships. It intends to add an interactive audio and video communications setup that will include a "what you see is what I see" CAD system so that an integrator and a customer do not have to be in the same place to collaborate on a design. And it plans to automate the access to its library so that integrators and customers— even on their own—can generate a wider range of designs and execute each one more quickly.

When Ross started down this road eight years ago, its primary goal was to gain customers for life by expanding the company's capabilities to meet each one's changing needs. It is clearly making a lot of progress. At a time when GM is reexamining virtually all its supplier relations, its Metal Fabricating Division won't go to any company but Ross for pneumatic valves and won't let its suppliers, either. Knight Industries, a supplier of ergonomic material-handling equipment, gives Ross 100% of its custom business and about 70% of its standard (catalog) business. When a competitor tried to woo Knight away, its president, James Zaguroli, Jr., responded, "Why would I switch to you? You're already five product generations behind where I am with Ross."

How Peapod Is Customizing the Virtual Supermarket

One company that is exploiting learning relationships in retailing services is Peapod, a grocery-shopping and delivery service based in Evanston, Illinois. Its customers—currently in Chicago and San Francisco—buy a software application for $29.95 that enables them to access Peapod's database through an online computer service. They then pay $4.95 per month for the service and a per-order charge of $5 plus 5% of the order amount. Peapod's back office is linked into the mainframe data-bases of the supermarkets at which it shops for its customers (Jewel in Chicago and Safe-way in San Francisco), allowing it to provide all the supermarkets' stock-keeping units and shelf prices electronically to its customers.

Rather than automating the trip to a retail store, as other on-line providers are doing, Peapod is using interactive technology to change the shopping experience altogether.

It lets each customer create the virtual super-market that best suits him or her. Using a personal computer, customers can shop in the way they prefer. They can request a list of items by category (snack foods), by item (potato chips), by brand (Frito-Lay), or even by what is on sale in the store on a given day. Within categories, they can choose to have the items arranged alphabetically by brand, by package size, by unit price, or even by nutritional value. Customers also can create and save for repeated use standard and special shopping lists (baby items, barbecue needs, and the like).

Peapod teaches its customers to shop so effectively in its virtual supermarket that most of them discover that—despite the company's rates—they *save* money because they use more coupons, do better comparison shopping, and buy fewer impulse items than they would if they shopped at a real supermarket. In addition, they save time and have more control over it because they can shop from home or work whenever they want.

Peapod has found that every interaction with a customer is an opportunity to learn. At the end of each shopping session, it asks the customer, "How did we do on the last order?" Peapod gets feedback on 35% of orders; most companies consider a 10% response rate to customer-satisfaction surveys to be good. And more than 80% of Peapod's customers have responded at one time or another. The feedback has prompted the company to institute a variety of changes and options, including providing nutritional information, making deliveries within a half-hour window (for an additional $4.95) rather than the usual 90-minute window, accepting detailed requests (such as three ripe and three unripe tomatoes), and delivering alcoholic beverages.

Peapod views delivery as another opportunity to learn about customers' preferences. It asks its deliverers to find out where customers would like the groceries left when they're not at home and anything else that will enhance the relationship. They fill out an "interaction record" for every delivery to track those preferences (as well as entering basic service metrics, such as the time of the delivery).

Even with the rates it charges, Peapod has to be efficient and effective to make money in what is a low-margin business. That is why it mass-customizes all shopping and delivery processes. Each order is filled by a generalist, who shops the aisles of the store, and as-needed specialists, who provide the produce, meats, deli, seafood, and bakery items to the generalist. The generalist pays for the groceries, often at special Peapod counters in the back of the store. The order is then taken to a holding area in the supermarket or in a trailer, where the appropriate items are kept cold or frozen until the deliverer picks up a set of orders and takes them to the customers. At each stage—ordering, shopping, holding, and delivery—the processes are modularized to provide personalized service at a relatively low cost.

If a customer has a problem, he or she can call Membership Services, and a service representative will try to resolve the matter. Peapod treats each call as yet another opportunity to learn (and remember) each customer's preferences and to figure out what the company can do to improve service for customers as a whole. For example, service representatives found that some customers were receiving five bags of grapefruits when they really wanted only five grapefruits. In response, Peapod now routinely asks customers to confirm orders in which quantities might be confused.

Peapod's results stand as a testament to the power of learning relationships. The four-year-old service, which has 7,500 customers and revenues of about $15 million, has a customer-retention rate of more than 80%. And the service accounts for an average of 15% of the sales volume of the 12 Jewel and Safeway stores where Peapod shops for its customers.

How to Interact: A Sampler of Today's Technologies

Interactive media that allow marketers to send specific messages to specific consumers and to conduct a dialogue with actual and potential customers already exist. One is the Internet, which now boasts more than 15 million users. Using it simply to prospect for customers remains problematic owing to the hostility of many users to commercial advertising on the Internet. But many companies have found the Internet to be a good way to obtain information from or about customers through bulletin boards, direct connections, and company-specific information services.

Other on-line services, such as those provided by Prodigy, America Online, and Compuserve, are much more advanced than the Internet in providing a full-fledged, structured medium through which customers and companies can interact. And several company-specific on-line services, such as grocery deliverer Peapod's, have proved useful for facilitating dialogues with customers.

Electronic kiosks have a wide variety of applications for interacting directly with customers. Some are purely informational—like those that provide directions to local spots from a hotel lobby. Others dispense coupons or gift certificates. And an increasing number are being used to dispense mass-customized products, including greeting cards, business cards, and sheet music.

A variety of interactive telephone services exists already. Seattle-based FreeFone Information Network offers one on the West Coast that enables marketers to find consumers willing to participate in a dialogue. When people sign up for the service, they fill out a questionnaire that is used to determine which advertiser's message is sent to which person. Each time a consumer makes a personal call and listens to a sponsored message while waiting for the call to connect, FreeFone credits the household account a nickel. The household gets a dime if the consumer requests more information, a coupon, or a telephone connection to the advertiser. Companies that advertise through FreeFone, including TicketMaster, the U.S. Postal Service, NBC, and the National Association of Female Executives, can learn a great deal about each household. But FreeFone will not divulge a caller's identity to an advertiser unless the caller chooses to reveal it.

Cash-back telephone coupons provide a similar way for companies and consumers to learn about each other over the phone. These services, offered by such companies as Chicago-based Scherers Communications, are essentially reverse 900 numbers. For example, a car manufacturer might credit someone $5 for watching a videotape touting some particular models and calling in with the personal identification number contained on the tape.

Fax response is being used by many business-to-business organizations and a small but growing number of consumer-goods manufacturers to give customers up-to-the-minute price quotations and product options. Fax response provides the marketer with the telephone-number identity of the individual who requested the information, which can be linked with transactional data as well as with mailing information.

R.R. Donnelley & Sons' selective binding technology, which enables printers to put different pages in different editions of a given publication, has made it possible for publishers to mass-customize periodicals. *Farm Journal*, for example, assembles information on individual subscribers—how many acres of what particular crops they have planted, how many head of cattle they own, and so on—and then uses Donnelley's technology to tailor the editorial content and the advertising of each edition for the particular subscriber.

ABOUT THESE AUTHORS

B. Joseph Pine II is cofounder of Strategic Horizons in Aurora, Ohio.

Don Peppers and *Martha Rogers* are founders of the Peppers & Rogers Group, a consultancy headquartered in Norwalk, Connecticut, specializing in customer relationships. Rogers is also an adjunct professor at Duke University's Fuqua School of Business.

ALSO BY THESE AUTHORS

B. Joseph Pine II
***Harvard Business Review* Articles**
"Four Faces of Mass Customization"
with James H. Gilmore

"Making Mass Customization Work"
with Bart Victor and Andrew C. Boynton
"Welcome to the Experience Economy"
with James H. Gilmore

Harvard Business Press Books
Authenticity: What Consumers Really Want
with James H. Gilmore

Also by These Authors

*Experience Economy: Work Is Theatre &
Every Business a Stage*
with James H. Gilmore

*Markets of One: Creating Customer-Unique
Value through Mass Customization*
with James H. Gilmore

*Mass Customization: The New Frontier in
Business Competition*

Don Peppers
Harvard Business Review Article
*"Is Your Company Ready for One-to-One
Marketing?"*
with Martha Rogers and Bob Dorf

Martha Rogers

Harvard Business Review Article

"*Is Your Company Ready for One-to-One Marketing?*"

with Don Peppers and Bob Dorf